Eco-Solutions:

It's In Your Hands

Oliver S. Owen

Published by Abdo & Daughters, 4940 Viking Drive, Suite 622, Edina, Minnesota 55435.

Library bound edition distributed by Rockbottom Books, Pentagon Tower, P.O. Box 36036, Minneapolis, Minnesota 55435.

Edited by Bob Italia

Cover photo credit: Stockworks
Inside photo credit: Peter Arnold - pgs. 6, 22, 47
      Stock Market - pgs. 8, 19, 21, 30, 32, 33, 43, 48
      Archive - pgs. 11
      AP/Wide World - pgs. 35, 27
      UPI/Bettmann - pgs. 17
      Allstock - pg. 49

Library of Congress Cataloging-In-Publication Data

Owen, Oliver S., 1920-
Eco-solutions: how we can make our sick earth well/ written by Oliver S. Owen.
p. cm. - (Target earth)
Includes glossary and index.
Summary: Discusses environmental problems including population growth, air and water pollution and the depletion of natural resources.
ISBN: 1-56239-203-4
1. Environmental degradation—Juvenile literature. 2. Sustainable development—Juvenile literature. 3. Environmental protection—Juvenile literature. [1. Environmental protection. 2. Conservation of natural resources.] I. Title. II Series.
GE14.5.094   1993
363.--dc20   93-19132
                                    CIP
                                    AC

About the Author

Oliver Owen is a Professor Emeritus for the University of Wisconsin at Eau Claire. His book *Natural Resource Conservation: An Ecological Approach* (Macmillan) is in its fifth edition. Dr. Owen has also written *Intro To Your Environment* (Abdo & Daughters Publishing) for the Target Earth Earthmobile environmental science program. He has a Ph.D. in Zoology from Cornell University.

Thanks to the trees from which this recycled paper was first made.

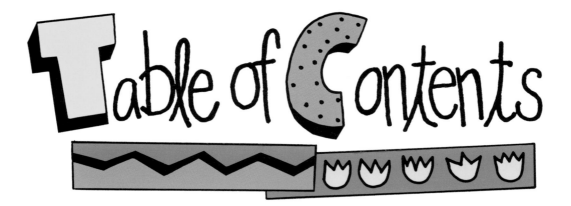

Table of Contents

An Intro To Environmental Science

What is the Environment?

Think for a moment. What or whom did you see on your way to school today? What or whom did you hear? What did you feel? What did you smell? Your list might include the following:

- You saw: houses, sidewalks, roads, bridges, fences, shops, sunshine, clouds, rain, smoke, rocks, soil, vegetable gardens, grass, dandelions, trees, ants, robins, sparrows, squirrels, dogs, cats, and people.

- You smelled: garbage, car exhaust, gasoline fumes, flowers, and perfume.

- You heard: the crash of thunder, the slap of rain on the windows, the moaning of the wind, the roar of traffic, the chirp of a robin, music on your car radio, the screeching of tires, the rustle of clothes, footsteps on the sidewalk, the laughter of your classmates, the roar of a lawnmower.

- You felt: the clothes on your body, the sidewalk under your feet, the wind on your face, the handlebars on your bike, the books under your arm, the warmth of the sun.

These things, which you saw, smelled, heard, or felt, formed part of your environment on your way to school today.

New York City is an environment to over 5 million people.

We can define environment as "the world around us." Even a volcanic eruption on an island in the Pacific or the destruction of a forest in South America can be considered part of your environment.

Your environment has living parts, such as dogs, birds and people. It also has non-living parts such as rocks, water, air and sunlight. These living and non-living parts affect each other in ways that are either beneficial or harmful to humans. We shall look at these interactions later.

What is Science?

When some students hear the word "science," they frown and say, "Yuk!" But science isn't dull at all. It can be very exciting—especially when it relates directly to your survival and health as a resident of planet Earth!

We can define science as "an organized body of knowledge about the world and its parts which is based on observations, hypothesis and experiments (hypothesis-testing)." Scientific studies are very orderly and precise.

Scientists first make careful observations, aided by instruments like microscopes, photometers or satellite-mounted cameras. Next they form hypotheses to explain what they see. They then test their hypothesis with experiments.

You may not realize it, but you are a scientist. You have been using the scientific method for much of your young life. Suppose that you have some pet goldfish. One day you make an observation: the fish look sick. You then make a hypothesis. "The goldfish are not getting enough oxygen from the water." To test your hypothesis, you conduct an experiment. You turn on an aerator and raise the level of oxygen in the water. The result? The goldfish become active. Your hypothesis was correct!

What is Environmental Science?

The study of environmental science provides humans with the proper prescriptions for making our "sick" planet well again. Environmental science examines how the living and non-living parts of the environment affect each other. The environmental scientist borrows from many other sciences like biology, chemistry, geology (study of rocks), climatology and the science of soils. It also deals with information from the fields of engineering, public health, sociology, forestry and agriculture. Although it covers many different topics, the major emphasis is always people: How can Earth's resources be used more effectively in promoting the quality of life for humans? Equally important to the environmental scientist is the question: How should humans behave so that our "sick" planet Earth will again be made well?

The environmental scientist is different from the astronomer who focuses his telescope on stars in his lonely mountaintop observatory. Instead, the environmental scientist is "where the action is"—trying to develop an understanding of the many environmental problems that face human society daily.

Environmental scientists are studying the question:
How can we make our "sick" Earth well again?

More and more, environmental scientists are offering urgent advice to government officials, industrial leaders, college professors, teachers, students and the public. They are providing the best approach to maintaining the "health" of both human society and the planet Earth on which that society depends.

Chapter 1

Why Our Earth Is Sick

Today, the environment of planet Earth is very sick. There are three major reasons:

- too many people;

- pollution of land, air and water;

- the overuse of natural resources.

Too Many People

You've seen them on national TV—thousands of African children slowly starving to death. You've seen the sunken eyes, the jutting ribs, and the stick-like limbs. You've seen the flies crawling over their bodies as life slips slowly away. This is a problem caused in part by overpopulation.

Well within your lifetime, the Earth's population will double from five billion to ten billion. At present rates of population growth, such doubling will occur every 41 years! During 1990, the global population increased at an annual rate of about 1.7 percent. That doesn't sound like much, does it? But think of all the wars America has ever fought—the Revolutionary War, the War of 1812, the Civil War, the Spanish-American War, World War I, World War II, the Korean War, the Viet Nam War, and the Gulf War. At the world's present rate of population growth, all the American soldiers killed in these wars could be replaced in only five days!

Overpopulation and starvation have become major environmental problems.

Because of the world's skyrocketing population, many poor nations are experiencing widespread starvation. There's just not enough food to go around. In the time it takes you to eat your noon lunch, 2,000 people somewhere on Earth will die because of empty stomachs! Worldwide, at least 42 million people die each year because of starvation, or disease resulting from poor nourishment.

From 1950 to 1984, the world's grain harvests grew three percent each year. However, since 1984, harvests have increased only one percent annually. In 1991, pollution and poor farming projects caused a $42 billion crop and livestock loss.

The careless, almost negative attitude toward population control is very discouraging. It certainly is a problem in America. In 1933, the U.S. population reached 256 million — an all-time high. In many poor nations of Africa, Asia and South America, the population is doubling every 20 years! There are 800 million women of child-bearing age. Three of every four of these women live in the poor or less-developed countries (LDCs). Only about 4 percent of African couples practice birth control. In India, the population increase between 1986 and 2000 is expected to be 230 million. That's almost equal to the total population of the United States!

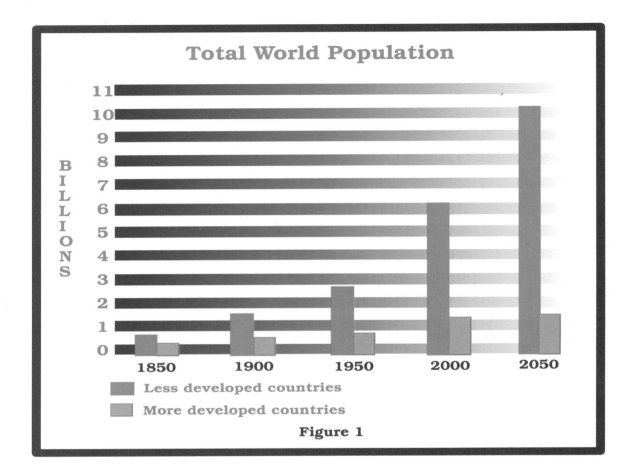

Total World Population

BILLIONS

1850   1900   1950   2000   2050

■ Less developed countries
■ More developed countries

Figure 1

In America, most elderly people have some sort of federal assistance such as Social Security and Medicare. They do not have to depend on their children. In LDCs, however, most people do not get such aid from the government. So, it is important for couples in these poor nations to have large families. Their children will serve as their "Social Security" and "Medicare" programs when they are old.

Another important reason for the population explosion in the LDCs is the high social status a man gets because he has fathered children. The greater the number of children, the bigger his "macho" image. In fact, a native of the African nation of Kenya recently boasted that during his lifetime, he had fathered more than 100 children! With attitudes like this, it is little wonder that population "bombs" are going off in many LDCs.

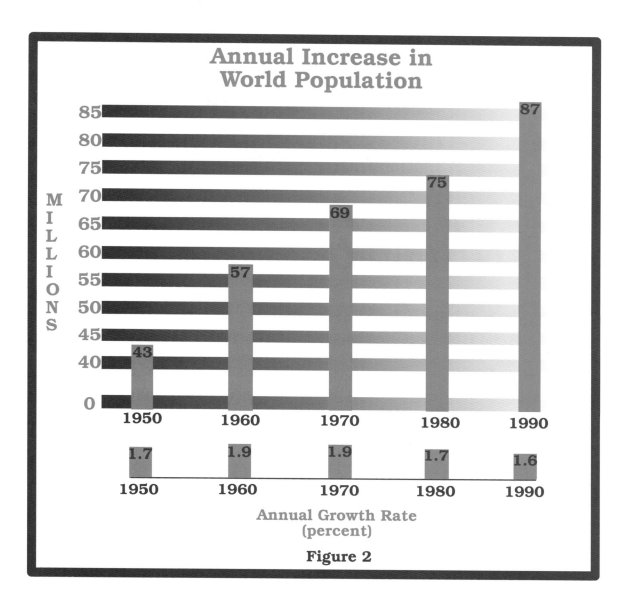

Annual Increase in World Population

Figure 2

What You Can Do

There are hungry people in your hometown, as well as in distant parts of the world like Somalia, Africa. You can help by donating a bag of groceries once a month to your local Salvation Army or similar relief agency.

13

Chapter 2
Environmental Pollution

Pollution and Solid Waste

They call the U.S. "America the Beautiful." But it's just not true. America is the world's champion producer of solid waste. America has only 5 percent of the world's population. But it forms a whopping 70 percent of its solid waste. That's about 14 times its fair share.

Just consider what's happening in the state of California. The 20 million Californians produce enough trash each year to form a mound 30 feet (9 meters) high and 100 feet (30 meters) wide. This mound would reach from Oregon all the way to Mexico! From 1965 to 2000, the United States will have produced about 10 billion tons of solid waste. Even if this stuff were pressed together, it would still fill a landfill (or "dump") the size of Delaware. Even worse, it would cost American taxpayers more than $500 billion just to bury the stuff!

The United States junks 55 billion cans every year. Americans throw cans away any old place. Beer cans are spotting the white "shoulders" of beautiful Mount Rainier in Washington. Soup cans bob in the canoe waters of Minnesota. Even parts of the California desert sparkle in the sun because of cans that were flung by absent-minded tourists.

As an environmental eyesore, a rusty tin can is bad enough. But how about a whole car? How about 7 *million* cars? That's the number that Americans were junking back in the 1960s. The value of a junked car in those days was about $5. It simply was not worth having it towed to the salvage yard. So countless car owners simply left their cars on the road where they had "conked out." Roughly 60,000 were abandoned yearly in New York City alone, and up to 200,000 nationwide. The rusty remains of old cars appeared everywhere—in backyards, vacant lots, and even in cemeteries!

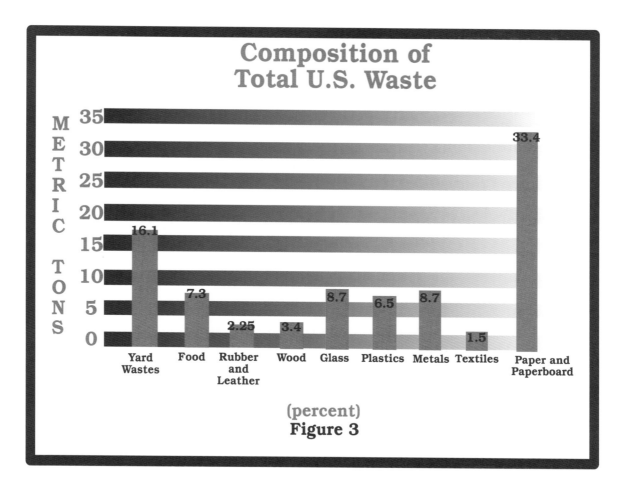

Composition of Total U.S. Waste

METRIC TONS

- Yard Wastes: 16.1
- Food: 7.3
- Rubber and Leather: 2.25
- Wood: 3.4
- Glass: 8.7
- Plastics: 6.5
- Metals: 8.7
- Textiles: 1.5
- Paper and Paperboard: 33.4

(percent)
Figure 3

Pollution and Hazardous Waste

A few years ago, I was driving through the lovely hills of northern Wisconsin. As I sped along, I suddenly noticed a column of dense smoke. It was black-brown and ugly against the milk-blue sky. Some-what curious, I traced the smoky flame to its source—a pile of burning tires in a nearby village dump. I was furious. Tire burning was against the law. But in the late 1970s, this was still a common method for get-ting rid of the 100 million tires discarded by American motorists each year.

What are hazardous wastes? They are the chemical waste products of industry that can be very harmful to humans. Many are very poisonous, and can cause serious illness and even death. For many years, the American public and its health agencies didn't worry too much about them. Much of this waste was buried or put in big metal containers and dumped at the edge of town, so these hazardous wastes were "out of sight and out of mind."

The Love Canal Disaster

Suddenly in 1977, an "alarm" went off. Hazardous chemicals began oozing out of a dump known as Love Canal near Niagara Falls, New York. Between 1947 and 1952, Hooker Chemical Company had dumped more than 20,000 tons of toxic water into the Love Canal. One chemical was dioxin. It causes cancer, and is one of the world's most deadly poisons. After dumping the waste, the Hooker Chemical Company capped it with a layer of soil.

In 1952, the city of Niagara Falls bought the dump site and the land around it. The city then built a brand new grade school on the property. Many homes were also built nearby. During the construction activity, several rusty barrels holding the hazardous waste were broken. A "witches brew" of poisonous chemicals bubbled up from the ground. An awful smell filled the air. Grade school students had to hold their noses on their way to class. After heavy rains, a "soup" of poisonous chemicals was washed into the basements of nearby homes. The school's play-ground became contaminated. So did backyard swimming pools. Bark peeled off once healthy trees. Flowers withered and died. Lawns turned a sickly brown.

In 1978, some soil, air, and water tests were made. The conclusion? At least 82 hazardous chemicals had escaped from the dump! The New York State Health Department then studied the health of the people in the area. The results were even more shocking. The study showed un-usually high rates of genetic damage, stillbirths (babies born dead), birth defects, lung disease, nervous disorders, kidney problems and cancer. President Jimmy Carter called Love Canal a federal disaster area. The state of New York helped 239 families find homes elsewhere. The grade school and all homes within 1-1/2 blocks of the dump were torn down. Health officials still are not sure what kind of illness the former school children of Love Canal might suffer in the future.

An aerial view of Niagara Falls, New York, shows the Love Canal chemical waste dump area. In 1977, hazardous chemicals began oozing out of the dump.

How to Control the Solid Waste Problem

In 1980, the U.S. government banned all open dumps. Since then, sanitary landfills have replaced the dumps. The landfill is an excavation into which solid wastes are dumped, compressed and covered with dirt. Since the wastes are not burned, air pollution is sharply reduced. Even more, the soil cover eliminates health problems caused by flies and rats. Once the landfill has been filled, the site can be used for other purposes, such as recreation. A good example is Mile-High Stadium in Denver, Colorado—the home of the Denver Broncos football team! Unfortunately, our nation is running out of places to put landfills. This is a serious problem, because by 1995 half of our 6,000 landfills will be filled up or closed.

Some garbage and scrap wood can be burned in incinerators—a specially designed furnace. The heat can be used to warm buildings, or to produce steam so that power plants can generate electricity.

Much "waste" is really not "waste" at all. It should be considered a valuable resource and be recycled. Much waste paper can be converted into cardboard or used in newspapers and books. (This book uses recycled paper!) Broken beer or catsup bottles will not disintegrate for at least a million years! If the U.S. government passes a law that requires people to recycle all used bottles, such a bill would save the energy-hungry nation at least 80,000 barrels of oil annually. It could save enough electricity to supply the needs of 1.5 million homes! Bottles can be crushed and used to make asphalt road pavement last longer. (Imagine thousands of cars speeding over broken glass!) Glass can be made into bricks and cinder-blocks.

In 1983, America was recycling only about 15 percent of the solid waste produced in its cities. However, only 10 years later (1993), more than 3,000 curbside recycling programs had been established. As a nation, Americans should try to recycle at least 80 percent of our urban solid waste. What a dent that would put in its land pollution problem!

What You Can Do
Form a litter clean-up patrol. Your motto can be "Every litter bit hurts!" Set up a schedule and post it on the bulletin board in your classroom. Once each week, a team of six students will remove all trash from the schoolyard. Place all recyclable materials like bottles, cans and paper in a special container. Ask your school custodian for the best method of disposal.

Recycling will help prevent pollution.

Pollution of the Water

In the past few decades, water pollution has caused many serious problems over much of this planet. Here are some that have occurred in the United States:

- maggot-infested fish rotting on a Lake Erie's beach;

- eight young people coming down with typhoid fever after eating a watermelon they found floating in the Hudson River;

- the Cuyahoga River in Ohio bursting into flames;

- 18,000 people in Riverside, California, stricken with fever and vomiting;

- 140 million fish killed in America's streams annually;

- 400 million tons of mud washed into the Gulf of Mexico by the Mississippi River each year;

- a high frequency of earthquake tremors near Denver, Colorado;

- the Mahoning River in Ohio heating up to 140 degrees Fahrenheit (60 degrees Centigrade)—warm enough to kill all fish;

- an outbreak of liver infections in people living in New York and New Jersey;

- the "death" of a lake near Santa Barbara, California;

- Many thousands of fish floating belly up in the Potomac River just below the U.S. Capitol.

These seemingly different types of problems had one thing in common—they were caused by water pollution. Let's look at three major kinds: sediment (or mud), disease organisms and oil.

140 million fish die every year in Americas streams from water pollution.

Sediment Pollution

You normally wouldn't think of soil as harmful. Farmers depend upon fertile soil to produce food to nourish hungry people. But suppose that heavy rains wash this very same soil into a stream or lake. Now it suddenly becomes a serious water pollutant. The Mississippi River alone washes 400 million tons of soil (sediment) into the Gulf of Mexico every year. To haul only one year's load would require a train of boxcars that would reach two and one-half times around the Earth at the equator. Sediment chokes up navigation channels so that they have to be dredged out at a multi-million dollar expense. Sediment covers the weed beds in lakes and streams where fish like to feed and breed. Some fish may even suffocate because sediment covers their gills and interferes with breathing.

Sometimes sediment will completely fill a lake and cause its "death." That's what happened to Lake Como in St. Paul, Minnesota. It began filling up with sediment in 1926. Only ten years later, this once beautiful body of water was "dead and buried." Generally, sediment pollution causes billions of dollars of damage in the United States each year. Yes, plain old mud ranks as our most destructive water pollutant!

How To Control Sediment Pollution

Farmers have traditionally plowed their land before planting their crops. This method left the soil bare, loose and open to erosion. But with special equipment that was recently developed, they can now inject seeds, fertilizer and weed-killing chemicals directly through the remains (leaves, stalks, etc.) of the previous crop. This process is called conservation tillage.

In 1993, more than 30 million acres of American farmland used conservation tillage. An experiment recently conducted in Georgia showed that this technique reduced soil erosion from 26 tons to only .1 ton per acre—much more than a 99 percent decrease!

At the beginning of the century, most farmers plowed up and downhill in straight rows. It was easy for rain water to wash the soil downhill into

Contour planting in Fall, Iowa.

nearby streams. Today, farmers plow around the hill—on the contour. The curving rows of crops are at right angles to the downhill flow of water. So soil erosion is reduced by 70 percent.

The farmer can plant alternate strips of cover crops, such as alfalfa, with row crops, like corn. The water flows easily downhill through the row crop but the dense stems of the cover crop check it. Loss of soil due to erosion can be reduced by 70 percent.

In this practice, cover crops and row crops are rotated on a given plot of land on an annual cycle. During much of the year, the cover crop protects some soil from erosion, thus reducing losses sharply.

What You Can Do

Make a soil erosion survey along the shores of a river or stream near your town. Take photographs of any sites where soil is being washed into the water. Pinpoint the exact location of the erosion. Notify your regional Soil Conservation Service office. Write a "letter to the editor" of your local newspaper and describe the erosion problem. You can also cover any bare spots in your lawn with sod.

The Invisible Enemy

About one of every five humans has access to safe drinking water. Water pollution is responsible for more human disease than any other environmental factor. Among the diseases it causes are cholera, typhoid fever, dysentery, infectious hepatitis, and polio. In 1990, more than 3.2 million children died from waterborne diarrhea disease alone. Most cases of these diseases occur in the less-developed countries of South America, Africa and Asia. In the United States, the death rate from each illness has dropped dramatically in the past century. The reason? Chlorination of drinking water and proper sewage treatment.

Two disease outbreaks in the United States were caused by microscopic organisms carried in polluted waters. In the early 1960s, some children were playing along the Hudson River in New York. At this time, four hundred million gallons of sewage was being discharged into the river everyday. One morning, the children spotted a watermelon floating down the river. They sliced it up and had a feast. Soon afterward, eight of the young people came down with typhoid fever.

Infectious hepatitis is a well-known disease that can be fatal to humans. It is caused by a waterborne virus (a microscopic organism). This virus causes damage to the liver. The symptoms of the disease include fever, extreme weakness, vomiting, yellow skin and coffee-colored urine.

Some years ago, an extensive outbreak of the disease took place in New York and New Jersey. Public health workers found something interesting: Each disease victim had eaten clams that were harvested from Reritan Bay, off the New Jersey coast. The clams had become infected with the virus while feeding in waters contaminated with human sewage.

During the early part of this century, Chicago, Illinois, discharged raw sewage into Lake Michigan. Unfortunately, Chicagoans also got their drinking water from the lake! You can guess the result: Thousands of people contacted typhoid fever and cholera. In just one epidemic, at least 80,000 people died—12 percent of the city's population!

How To Control Disease Organism Pollution

These disease outbreaks took place some years ago. Proper treatment of drinking water and sewage has sharply reduced the problem in the United States. Still, waterborne diseases made at least 100,000 Americans very sick between 1975 and 1993.

In the poor nations of Africa, Asia and South America, sewage and drinking water is not properly treated. The result? Typhoid and cholera are killing more than 25,000 people every day!

In 1974, the U.S. Congress passed the Safe Drinking Water Act. It established purity standards for the nation's drinking water. Under this act, all water supplies must be chlorinated to destroy infectious bacteria.

Human wastes undergo treatment at more than 13,000 plants throughout the United States. Before being discharged into lakes and streams, the treated sewage is also chlorinated. This is important because some city downstream from the plant may use the water for drinking purposes!

About one in every 20 Americans do not trust public water sources. Instead, they purchase bottled water at supermarkets. The cost? About $1.25 per gallon (4 liters).

What You Can Do

Dozens of viruses in drinking water are not destroyed by routine chlorination. Write a letter to your local and state health and water departments urging them to develop methods to remove all viruses from drinking water.

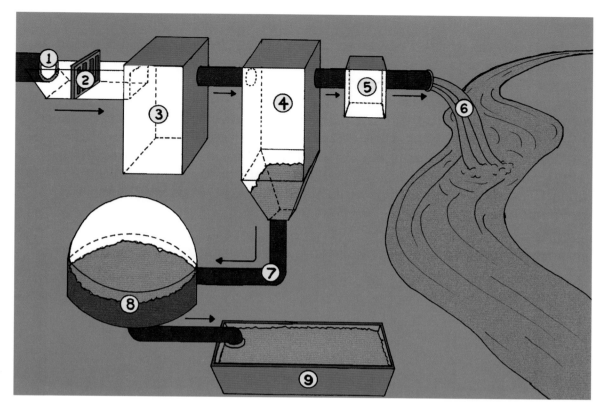

Sewage Treatment Plant

1. Raw sewage from sewer.
2. Bar screen removes large debris.
3. Grit chamber where grit settles to bottom.
4. Settling tank where heavy particles settle and form sludge.
5. Chlorination tank kills bacteria.
6. Treated water is discharged into river.
7. Sludge collects and travels to the sludge digester (8).
8. Sludge is digested by bacteria.
9. Sludge is pumped into a sludge drying bed where it will eventually be used as fertilizer.

Oil

In 1989, the United States experienced its greatest oil pollution disaster. A huge Exxon oil tanker hit a reef and broke up in stormy seas in Prince William Sound, near Valdez, on the south coast of Alaska. The tanker's hull was ripped open. More than 11 million gallons of heavy crude oil escaped into the sea. Brown-black fuel quickly covered more than 1,400 miles of coastline. Thousands of sea birds, otters and seals died. Valuable salmon fisheries went out of business. Eventually in 1993, the Exxon Oil Company paid the state of Alaska $1 billion in damages. The total environmental damage caused by the spill is yet to be determined.

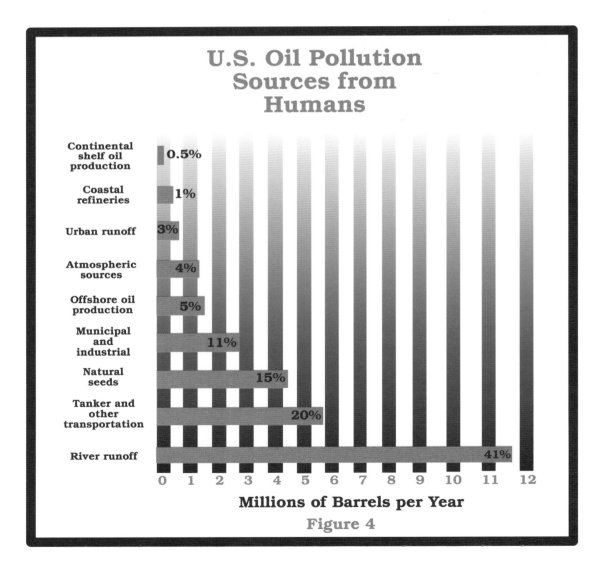

Figure 4

The Exxon Valdez *oil tanker (bottom ship) spilled 11 million gallons of crude oil into Prince William Sound, Alaska.*

How To Control Oil Pollution

Tougher government standards for American-owned oil tankers have been established since 1980. New tankers must be equipped with back-up radar and back-up steering controls. If a reef-crack-up knocks out one steering mechanism, another can get the ship out of dangerous waters. This is important because some giant tankers are more than one-quarter mile long and are as wide as a football field. Inspection of American tankers has been more frequent and more demanding.

Inspection should not be limited just to the tankers. The procedures for loading and unloading oil should be examined more closely. Training of the tanker crews should be upgraded. Even more, the ocean routes used by oil tankers should be closely regulated so that the possibility of tanker break-ups is sharply reduced.

What You Can Do

Write a letter to the National Oceanic and Atmospheric Administration (see Connect With Groups in the back of the book). Request upgrading of standards as shown in the last paragraph.

Air Pollution

To stay alive, you have to breathe in and out about once every four seconds. That's 16 times a minute, 960 times an hour, 23,040 times per day and 8,409,600 times each year! If you live to be 70 years old, you will inhale about 75 million gallons (37.5 liters) of air! That's why clean air is necessary for health and even life itself.

We have done a good job of polluting it. And this pollution is killing more than 53,000 Americans each year! It also causes serious damage to crops, trees and buildings—about $100 billion annually throughout the world.

Let's look at the causes and effects of two major types of air pollution—ozone and carbon monoxide.

Too Much Ozone

As motor vehicles speed along the road and highways, a "witches brew" of gases spew from engines and exhaust pipes. Under the influence of sunlight, these gases (hydrocarbons and nitrogen oxides) undergo a series of chemical reactions. As a result, a brownish haze is formed. It is known as photochemical smog or ozone. This smog can be found in cities such as Los Angeles, Denver, Salt Lake City and Mexico City. Peak levels in Los Angeles usually occur about 10 a.m. Ozone is very destructive to plants. It has caused many millions of dollars in damage to garden vegetables and ornamental flowers in California and along the East Coast.

Photochemical smog or ozone can be found in cities like Los Angeles and Denver. In Los Angeles, peak levels of smog usually occur about 10 a.m. In addition to being a human health hazard, ozone is very destructive to plants.

Ozone also causes major pine forest damage. It has shortened the life span of rubber products such as tires and windshield wipers. Any new resident of Los Angeles soon becomes aware of the "burning throat" and the "stinging eyes" caused by ozone. Even worse, ozone causes human sickness and death.

One such illness is bronchitis, characterized by breathing difficulties and a chronic cough. Another ozone-caused disease is emphysema. Ozone breaks down the lungs' air sacks which results in oxygen deficiency in the blood stream. At least 1.5 million Americans die from emphysema every year—more than from lung cancer and tuberculosis combined.

Not Enough Ozone

We have just learned that too much ozone at eye and nose levels can cause serious illness. On the other hand, too little ozone—high in the atmosphere—can also cause health problems.

Under normal conditions, a dense layer of ozone blankets the Earth at a height of 10-20 miles. It forms a protective shield against ultra-violet (short wave) radiation from the sun. Unfortunately, the world's industrialized nations, including the United States and Canada, are producing chemicals which are destroying the ozone shield. These chemicals are called chlorofluoron carbons or CFCs. CFCs are used in air conditioners and refrigerators. They also have been used to propel deodorants, insecticides, and shaving cream from spray cans. The Dupont chemical company produces $600 million worth of CFCs every year.

How do the CFCs get 10-20 miles above the Earth? Suppose that a few years ago, your dad sprayed foamy shave cream on his beard. Sooner or later, the CFC molecules escaped through the bathroom window and into the atmosphere. They then gradually rose above the tree tops and high into the sky. Eventually, they entered the ozone layer. These chemicals then underwent a series of chemical reactions that punched holes in the ozone blanket.

Scientists first became aware of this problem in 1979. They discovered a gigantic hole in the ozone layer over Antarctica. In spring, the ozone layer was only half as thick as it was in 1978. In 1988, a similar hole was found over the Arctic. Any thinning of the ozone shield will result in more intense ultra violet radiation from the sun. Physicians estimate that this would cause at least 1.4 million extra cases of skin cancer the world over. Many more people would suffer from cataracts— the clouding of the lens which causes blurred vision. Fish populations would decrease. Production of cotton, corn, and wheat would decline. This would cause financial hardship for farmers throughout the world.

How To Control Ozone Pollution

Control of the CFC pollution problem will be difficult. In 1987, the major CFC-producing nations met in Montreal, Ontario, Canada. They agreed to cut their CFC production 50 percent by 1999. The Dupont company has decided to stop CFC manufacturing altogether by the year 2000.

What You Can Do

Avoid spray can use.

Give a report on the CFC pollution problem to your class, or at a Boy Scout, Girl Scout, or 4-H meeting.

Write to your state and federal legislators urging tighter controls of CFC production.

Carbon Monoxide & the Greenhouse Effect

This gas is an invisible killer. We cannot see it, taste it or smell it. Yet it forms more than half our air pollution. It comes from the incomplete burning of fuel.

More than 90 percent of carbon monoxide comes from the exhaust pipes of cars, buses, trucks and other motor vehicles of big cities like New York, Chicago and Los Angeles. Large amounts of carbon monoxide also are released from the smoke stacks of power plants and factories, and from home chimneys. There is much of this gas even in cigarette smoke. A person who smokes a pack of cigarettes each day probably breathes in twice as much carbon monoxide than if he were a non-smoker and lived permanently in downtown New York!

Carbon monoxide is the cause of more than half our air pollution. More than 90 percent of carbon monoxide comes from the exhaust pipes of cars, buses, trucks and other motor vehicles.

Carbon monoxide is poisonous because it interferes with the blood's ability to feed oxygen to the body's cells. This causes oxygen starvation. A high level of carbon monoxide poisoning can result in death. But even lower levels can make a person sick. It worsens the condition of people suffering from asthma, tuberculosis or pneumonia. It increases the risk of heart attacks. Carbon monoxide will interfere with the ability of a driver to use his brakes or estimate the speed and distance of an oncoming car. This invisible gas probably kills many Americans because of traffic accidents every year—and many more worldwide.

How To Control Carbon Monoxide Pollution

A 1977 amendment to the U.S. Clean Air Act required all motor vehicles in the United States to use *catalytic converters.* This device looks like a muffler and weighs 10 to 30 pounds (4.5-13.5 kg). It is part of a car's exhaust system. One type, used by Ford Motor Company, has a honeycomb-shaped interior. Metal platinum lines the honeycomb's "cells." As carbon monoxide (CO) passes through the converter, the platinum increases the rate at which the carbon monoxide is "burned up" (combined with oxygen). The oxidation of the poisonous carbon monoxide forms harmless carbon dioxide (CO_2). Since catalytic converters were introduced, the carbon monoxide levels in America's major cities have gone down sharply.

But there is a way to decrease carbon monoxide levels even more. We can cut down on the total volume of motor vehicle exhaust. This can be done by:

   Relying more on public mass transit like buses and trains. (We would have to end our "love affair" with our private motor car!)

   Improving the fuel efficiency of cars from 30 miles (50 km) per gallon (5 L) to 50 miles (80 km) per gallon (5 L) by the year 2000.

   Shifting to fuels like natural gas and alcohol that are less polluting than gasoline.

   Shifting from gasoline-burning engines to cars powered by electricity, steam, or the sun.

The carbon dioxide (CO$_2$) in the air acts like the glass of a greenhouse. It allows sunlight to pass through it. However, it blocks heat rays from escaping into outerspace. Since 1860, atmospheric CO$_2$ has risen by 20 percent. This increase has largely been due to the increased burning of fuels like coal, oil and natural gas. In recent years, the burning of tropical rainforests in Central and South America and southeast Asia has contributed to the CO$_2$ build-up.

Scientists estimate that if CO$_2$ levels continue to rise at current rates, the average temperature of Earth will increase by 5 degrees Fahrenheit (3 degrees Celsius) by 2030. As a result, the polar ice caps and mountain glaciers will melt. This would cause the oceans to rise 3.3 feet (1m) by 2030. Then the seas would move more than 100 feet (30m) inland along our Atlantic and Gulf coasts. Massive flooding would occur in Boston, Philadelphia, New York City, Baltimore, Washington, Norfolk, Miami and New Orleans. Property damage would be measured in the billions.

America's wheat farmers would suffer a $500 million annual loss because of the increased warmth. Many of the world's best rice-growing regions would be destroyed by salt water. One-fifth of the most heavily populated areas of India and Bangladesh would be flooded. In short, the global warming by 2030 would cause immense property damage, agricultural losses, and severe economic hardships for millions of people worldwide.

The Bhopal Disaster

On December 3, 1984, one of the most serious cases of air pollution ever recorded occurred in Bhopal, India. It happened at an American-owned Union Carbide plant that manufactured a highly poisonous chemical used in pesticides. This chemical accidentally leaked from a huge storage tank and escaped into the atmosphere. Even worse, it happened during the middle of the night when most people were asleep. Many never woke up.

The toxic gas killed more than 2,500 in a very short time. It also caused injury to more than 500,000 Bhopal residents. Doctors predict at

In Bhopal, India, thousands of people were stricken when poisonous gas leaked from a Union Carbide pesticide factory.

least 100,000 members of this Indian city will suffer from brain damage, go blind, have serious liver and kidney infections, become sterile, or develop other major health problems.

The Spread of Air Pollution

Once pollutants are released into the atmosphere, they don't always stay in a small area near the source. They may move upward into the sky or spread out in all directions. A large variety of pollutants has "belched" from the smoke stacks of thousands of factories in the United States, Canada and Mexico for many years. Some of this aerial garbage is still in the air, high over our heads. How do we know? Just ask some American space scientists. They were shocked when they looked down toward planet Earth in 1992 and saw a huge orange-brown cloud of pollution. It was more than five miles thick. Even worse, this cloud of pollution covered an area larger than the entire continent of North America!

The Pollutions Standards Index

The U.S. Federal government developed the Pollutions Standards Index (PSI) in 1976. The index compares the air quality of different urban areas and the possible threat to human health.

A PSI rating of 100 is given to a city if the pollutants in the air are at acceptable levels. Any rating below 100 suggests clean air with little health effects. As the rating rises above 100, the air is more polluted and the health effects worsen. A PSI rating of 400 or greater suggests that air pollution is very hazardous. It may cause serious problems with the sick and elderly. When hazardous conditions exist, everyone should remain indoors.

How to reduce pollution from your family car

Persuade your family to:

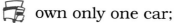 own only one car;

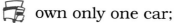 drive more slowly;

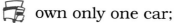 take shorter and fewer vacation trips by car;

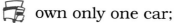 use mass transit (buses and trains);

 get the car tuned up regularly;

 do more walking and biking for trips under one mile.

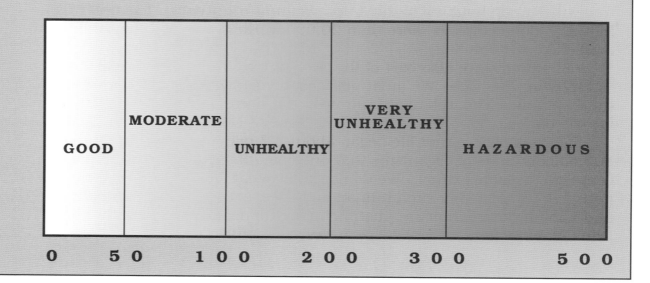

POLLUTIONS STANDARDS INDEX

GOOD   MODERATE   UNHEALTHY   VERY UNHEALTHY   HAZARDOUS

0   5 0   1 0 0   2 0 0   3 0 0   5 0 0

How to Reduce Pollution from Electric Power Plants that Burn Oil or Coal

Persuade your family to:

- keep the thermostat at 70 degrees Fahrenheit (20°C) or less;

- put on sweaters instead of turning up the heat;

- turn the thermostat down to 60 degrees Fahrenheit (15°C) when leaving the house;

- use a new type of energy-efficient lightbulb;

- turn off all lights when leaving a room.

Wildlife Depletion

Our wild animals, or wildlife, are valuable to us in many ways. Their behavior pleasantly stimulates us. Have you thrilled to the howl of a wolf? Have you seen the plunge of a fish hawk? Such events will live in your memory forever.

Our wildlife resource has scientific value. At any big university, you can take courses in everything from Animal Behavior to Wildlife Ecology. Our wild animals are valuable as a food source. Just ask anyone who has feasted on rabbit stew, broiled trout or venison.

Our wildlife resource has great recreational and economic values. America's hunters spend more than $1 billion annually on everything from rifles and shotguns to duck decoys and turkey calls. The firearms industry alone employs more than 20,000 workers and has a payroll of more than $100 million.

Wild animals are also part of the "web of life." They form important "strands" in this web. We must not foolishly cause the extinction of these strands. The web might unravel. If it does, the quality of human life will suffer.

Biologists believe that life began about 3.7 billion years ago. Of the 500 million kinds of organisms that once populated the Earth, 95 percent have become extinct. We do not know what caused those extinctions. However, today such human activities as economic development and habitat destruction are pushing many thousands of species to the brink of extinction.

When we consider all forms of life, including both plants and animals, one species is disappearing forever every day. However, if present habitat destruction rates continue, especially in the rainforests, one kind of plant or animal will become extinct every hour by the year 2000! Such a tremendous loss of biological diversity could not be repaired for millions of years.

How to Control Wildlife Depletion

The best way to upgrade our wildlife population is to preserve and improve their *habitat* — the natural places where they live. It is the animals' habitat that provides a food source, breeding sites, and protection from the weather.

Oil tanker spills have seriously damaged the sea coast habitat of many marine animals. A big spill, like the Shetland Island spill off northern Scotland in 1993, attracts worldwide attention. But there are hundreds of lesser spills every year. Together, these spills destroy hundreds of thousands of sea birds and mammals annually. To prevent future spills, tankers must undergo better inspection to make sure they are sea worthy. And the training of tanker crews must be upgraded.

Almost half of America's original duck marshes have been destroyed because of draining by farmers and housing developers. So, waterfowl populations have dropped sharply. Laws must be passed that make such draining illegal.

The Peregrine Falcon

Peregrine falcons have nested on cliff ledges for probably thousands of years. These fascinating birds, the swiftest in North America, were almost extinct a decade ago. American scientists have recently helped birds breed successfully in a completely different type of habitat. In fact, scientists have trained them to nest on the rooftops of skyscrapers!

In 1992, a pair of falcons nested on top of the MultiFoods building in downtown Minneapolis. Falcons have also been nesting on top of a classroom building at the University of Wisconsin in Madison. Other peregrines have nested on skyscraper rooftops in Baltimore, Maryland, and Milwaukee, Wisconsin.

"But what do these city falcons eat?" you ask. "There are no wild ducks flying over downtown city streets." The answer is simple. The birds shifted to a diet of pigeons! Now thousands of city dwellers can thrill to the spectacular sight of a "dive-bombing" falcon while waiting for the bus! But even more, the falcons are providing a great environmental service. They are keeping the pigeon population down.

*A female peregrine falcon feeds her one-week-old eyases on the
33rd floor ledge of the USF&G building in Baltimore.*

The Endangered Species Act

Habitat preservation and development is an excellent way to protect
our wildlife resource. Another important strategy is the enactment of
appropriate laws. One of the most successful U.S. laws is the 1974
Endangered Species Act.

This is how it works. Whenever scientists figure out that an animal
species is "endangered," it automatically receives protection from the
U.S. Department of Interior. (The "endangered" status is given to wildlife
species if it is faced with extinction because of habitat destruction, disease or predation.) This act protects about 758 animal species. Among
them are the grizzly bear, timber wolf and the peregrine falcon. Endangered species are protected from hunters or trappers. And their habitat
is carefully preserved, especially from dams, highways, houses and air-
ports.

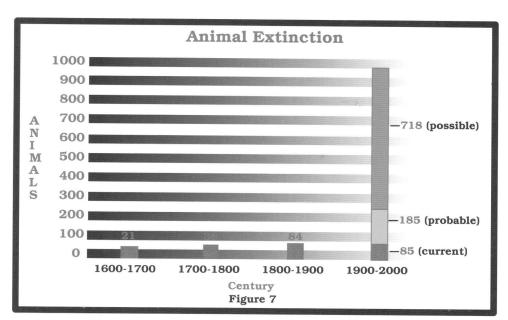

Animal Extinction

718 (possible)

185 (probable)

85 (current)

21

84

1600-1700   1700-1800   1800-1900   1900-2000

Century
Figure 7

Suppose that a hunter kills a wolf because it was mistaken for a coyote. Or suppose that a hunter shot a grizzly bear just for the "thrill of it." In each case, the sportsman could be fined $20,000 and sentenced to one year in a federal jail!

What You Can Do

📖 Convert your backyard into good wildlife habitat by planting trees and food plants.

📖 Operate a winter bird feeder. Keep it well stocked with cracked corn, sunflower seeds, millet and suet.

📖 If you are a Boy or Girl Scout, do your best to get a merit badge in Bird Study.

📖 With your parents' help, build nesting boxes for woodpeckers, bluebirds, chickadees, owls and wrens. Erect them in appropriate habitats.

📖 If a relative or friend owns property with wetlands, persuade him or her not to drain the land for farming or real estate purposes. Keep it in its natural state as prime wildlife habitat.

📖 Write to the U.S. Fish and Wildlife Service for more information on the Endangered Species Act (see *Connect With Groups* in the back of this book).

Chapter 3
Our Natural Resources

What is a natural resource? It is "any material produced by nature, which is valuable to human society." There are two major types of resources: renewable and non-renewable.

Renewable resources can be renewed by nature in a somewhat short time and again be available for human use. Soil, grasslands, forests, fish and wildlife are renewable resources.

Suppose that this very moment, thousands of pine seedlings began to grow behind your school. Only 80 years from now (if you did not trample those young trees while playing softball), they could develop into a valuable stand of mature pine.

Let's consider the most valuable game animal in North America—the white-tailed deer. Because of their great reproductive abilities, a herd of only six deer can grow to 1,000 head in only ten years. Similarly, a small population of bass or salmon can grow to many times its original size in a very short time.

Non-renewable resources cannot be renewed by nature rapidly enough to be useful to humans. Good examples are the so-called *fossil fuels:* coal, oil and natural gas. The energy in these fuels was derived from the sunlight that shone on plants living millions of years ago. These plants changed the solar energy to the chemical energy they needed to stay alive. Certain animals fed on these plants. After these plants and animals died, many tons of mud covered them. Movements of the Earth gradually subjected them to a great amount of heat and pressure. The result? Fossil fuels.

Without coal, oil and natural gas as sources of abundant energy, the quality of life enjoyed in Canada and America would come to a screeching halt. Unfortunately, once these fuels are used up, they are gone forever. Think about that the next time you turn up your thermostat on a cold winter night!

All metals, such as copper, iron, lead, aluminum and zinc are also non-renewable. Like fossil fuels, they too should be carefully conserved. After all, if we were suddenly deprived of them, our way of life would become primitive.

An aluminum manufacturing plant.

Approaches Toward Resource Use

Over the past two centuries, America has used three major approaches in its resource use:

 exploitation

 preservation

 ecological

The Exploitation Approach

This approach was very common in America's history. The exploiters would simply use a given resource such as timber, grasslands, soil, fish and wildlife as quickly as possible. The only concern was how much and how soon would the exploiter benefit.

The early loggers of the 1800s followed one basic rule: Get into the forest, log off the trees, then get out. And when they got out, nothing was left but stumps. Game hunters would shoot as many grouse, ducks, elk, deer and bear as they could, no matter whether these animals were rearing young or not. An old photo from the early 1900s shows two waterfowl hunters with their boats almost sinking from the weight of more than 100 dead ducks! Why shouldn't they kill as many as they could? There were no bag limits or game wardens to worry about.

Let's look at two of America's most dramatic examples of how exploitation can quickly destroy a once valuable resource.

The Dust Bowl

The cattle industry boomed in the Great Plains at the turn of the century. Livestock assumed the ecological role that antelope and buffalo filled for centuries. Waves of farmers crossed the Mississippi and took title to land granted by the federal government. Because of the nation's mushrooming population, there was great pressure on these ranchers and farmers for meat and grain.

Eager to make big profits, many ranchers crowded too many cattle on too small a range for too long a time. So, the native grasses began to wither, especially during years of drought.

The farmers sliced deep into the prairie sod with their new steel plows. They turned up the dark soil, and exposed it to the burning prairie sun. Only a few decades before, this upturned earth trembled under pounding buffalo hooves. The farmers planted wheat in the North and cotton in the South.

For years, both ranchers and farmers were successful. But then came the Big Drought. From 1926 to 1931, there was hardly enough rain to settle the dust. On the ranches, the buffalo grass and other prairie grasses withered and died. Scrawny cattle clipped overstocked pastures to ground level. Much livestock was mercifully slaughtered. Drought had visited the plains before. So had wind storms. But never in the history of the North American prairie was the land more vulnerable to their combined attack. Gone were the branching root systems of the prairie grasses that had once kept the rich brown soil firmly in place. On the ranches, the soil broke down from the pounding of millions of cattle.

44

On the wheat and cotton farms, the huge machinery used in plowing, cultivating and harvesting broke down the soil. The stage was set for the "black blizzards."

In the spring of 1934 and again in 1935, very strong winds swept over the Great Plains. In western Kansas and Oklahoma, and in the neighboring parts of Texas, Colorado, and Nebraska, the wind swirled tiny soil particles high into the prairie sky. Brown dust clouds up to 7,000 feet (2,133 m) thick filled the air. Their tops reached as high as two miles (3.3 km). One storm on May 11, 1934, lifted 300 million tons (272 metric tons) of fertile soil into the air. (This roughly equals the total soil tonnage scooped from Central America to form the Panama Canal.) In many areas, the wilted wheat was uprooted and blown into the air. In the Amarillo, Texas, area during the spring of 1935, fifteen wind storms raged for twenty-four hours. Four lasted over fifty-five hours.

Dust from Oklahoma prairies came to rest on the deck of a steamer 200 miles (322 km) out in the Atlantic. It sifted into the plush New York City offices of Wall Street. It smudged the luxury apartments of Park Avenue. When it rained in the blow area, the drops would sometimes come down as mud. In Washington, D.C., mud splattered buildings of the Department of Agriculture. It was a rude reminder of the problem facing the nation.

In 1934-35, strong winds swept over the Great Plains. Fertile soil was carried into the air and the southwestern United States became a "dust bowl."

A thousand miles westward, frantic homemakers stuffed water-soaked newspapers into window cracks. The dust sifted into kitchens. It formed a thin film on pots and pans and fresh-baked bread. Blinded by swirling dust clouds, ranchers got lost in their backyards. Motorists pulled off to the side of the highways. Hundreds of airplanes were grounded. Trains were stalled by huge dirt drifts. Hospital nurses placed wet cloths on patients' faces to ease their breathing. In Colorado (March 1935), forty-eight relief workers contracted "dust pneumonia." Four of them died. Five infants belonging to a New Mexico mother smothered to death in their cribs.

When the winds finally quieted down, ranchers and farmers wearily examined the damage. Millions of tons of fertile soil had been carried to the Atlantic seaboard. The coarser sand, too heavy to be airborne, bounced across the land and sheared off young wheat. Sand buried heavily mortgaged power machinery.

The dust storms of the 1930s caused both social and economic suffering. Yet a few ranchers and farmers were philosophical about their misfortunes. They even cracked jokes about the birds flying backward "to keep the sand out of their eyes," and about the prairie dogs "digging burrows 100 feet (30 m) in the air."

But for most Dust Bowl victims, the dusters were not very funny. Many were almost penniless. The 300 million tons (272 metric tons) of topsoil removed in a single storm on May 11, 1933, was equal to taking 3,000 farms of 100 acres 40 hectares each out of crop production. Dust Bowl relief until 1940 alone cost American taxpayers over $1 billion.

Many of these unlucky farmers had to find a new way of life. They piled their belongings into rickety cars and trucks and moved out. Some went to the Pacific coast, some to the big industrial cities of the Midwest and East. But America was still in the throes of a depression. Many of these people had found nothing but frustration, bitterness, and suffering at the end of the road.

The Passenger Pigeon

The passenger pigeon was once the most abundant bird on Earth. Early in the nineteenth century, Alexander Wilson, a famous bird watcher, saw a migrating flock that streamed past him for several hours. Wilson estimated the single flock to be one mile (1.6 km) wide and 240 miles (386 km) long and made up of about 2 billion birds. (The population of this flock was roughly ten times the total North American waterfowl population of today.) Yet not one passenger pigeon is left on this planet.

What factors contributed to the passenger pigeon's extinction? First, many potential nest and food trees (beech, maple, oak) were chopped down or burned to make room for farms and settlements. The pigeon fed extensively on beech nuts and acorns. The single flock seen by Wilson could have eaten 17 million bushels per day.

Second, disease may have taken a heavy toll. The breeding birds were susceptible to disease epidemics because they nested in dense colonies. In 1871, a concentration of 136 million pigeons nested in an 850-square-mile (2,236-square-km) region in central Wisconsin. A single tree had up to 100 nests.

Third, many pigeons may have been destroyed by severe storms during the long migration between the North American breeding grounds and the Central and South American winter home. Once a huge flock of young passenger pigeons flew into Crooked Lake, Michigan, after becoming blinded by a dense fog. Thousands drowned and lay a foot deep along the shore for miles.

The extinct passenger pigeon.

Fourth, the low breeding potential may have been a factor in their extinction. Many perching birds, such as robins, lay four to six eggs per clutch. Ducks, quail, and pheasants lay eight to twelve eggs. But the female pigeon produced only a single egg per nesting.

Fifth, market hunters destroyed many pigeons. They slaughtered the birds on their nests. Every imaginable method of destruction was employed, including guns, dynamite, clubs, nets, fire, and traps. One pass of the net caught over 1,300 birds. Pigeons were burned and smoked out of the nesting trees. Shot riddled migrating flocks. In one small Wisconsin village, pigeon hunters bought over sixteen tons (14.5 metric tons) of shot in a single year.

The fancy restaurants of Chicago, Boston, and New York considered pigeon flesh a tasty and fashionable dish. Each bird sold for 2 cents. In 1861, Petoskey, Michigan, shipped almost 15 million pigeons from a single nesting area. The last wild pigeon was shot in 1900. Martha, a lone captive survivor, died on September 1, 1914, at the age of twenty-nine, in the Cincinnati Zoo.

The Preservation Approach

The preservation approach suggests that some of our natural resources, such as forests and certain scenic wonders, should be kept intact for all time. In the late 1800s, the well-known naturalist, John Muir, proposed that some of America's unique woodlands should be set aside as National Parks. Logging, hunting, grazing and mining would be barred forever. The forest would remain a wilderness. As a National Park, its natural beauty could be enjoyed by visitors from all over the United States, and even the world, for centuries to come. (For more information, see the Target Earth Earthmobile book *Earth Keepers*.)

In 1890, the U.S. Congress established Yosemite National Park as a protected national forest.

Largely because of John Muir's urging, in 1890 the U.S. Congress established Yosemite National Park. It is in California, 200 miles (322 km) east of San Francisco, in the heart of the Sierra Nevada Mountains. Park visitors can hike along more than 700 miles (1,126 km) of natural trails. They can thrill to the sign of spectacular waterfalls, rugged mountain peaks, 200 kinds of birds, 1,300 kinds of plants, and a large number of bear and deer.

Yosemite is famous for its Sequoias or Big Trees. One of them, known as the "Grizzly Giant," has a diameter of over 34 feet (10 m)! And it is more than 2,000 years old! By 1990, a full century after Yosemite came into being, Congress had established 336 additional national park systems.

The Ecological Approach

The ecological approach to resource management is a major thrust of this book. In one sense, "ecology" is simply a fancy name for environmental science. Ecology can be defined as "the study of inter-relationships between organisms and their environment." One might also define ecology as the study of the "balance of nature" or the "web of life." Ecology tells us that we are not *masters* of nature but are *part* of nature. Humans fit into nature and must be in harmony with it.

How would a forest be managed from an ecological approach? The forest manager would use a concept known as *multiple use.* In other words, the forest has many more functions than merely serving as a source of timber.

Forest managers need to find a balance in nature so that our old growth forests are protected.

Suppose that the forest manager is debating whether she should log off all the mature pine trees on a certain mountain slope. Since she is using an ecological approach, she might ask: "If I log off these trees, how will other resources such as soil, water, air, fish and wildlife be affected? Will the result be helpful or harmful to human society?" The logging operation would provide more wood with which to build homes, shops, and bridges. It would also produce a variety of products from toothpicks to telephone poles.

But from an ecological standpoint, the logging operation might have some drawbacks:

The forest acts like a living sponge. It soaks up water during a heavy rain. Later it slowly releases the water to the farms and ranches in the valley below. Farmers make use of the water to irrigate their crops. Ranchers use it for their livestock. Once the trees are harvested, this living sponge would be gone. Water would rush down the slope after a heavy rain and be wasted. By late summer, both livestock and crops would suffer. Even worse, severe flooding could cause property damage and even loss of life.

The rapidly flowing runoff water could cause serious soil erosion. After all, the soil would be somewhat exposed at the logging site. The muddy water would then pollute the trout stream that flows through the valley. The sediment could kill large numbers of trout by clogging up their gills and making it impossible for them to get oxygen. Anglers would have to find another stream in which to enjoy their favorite sport.

The forest provides food, water, and breeding sites for wildlife such as grouse, eagles, deer and bear. It also gives them protection from wind, cold, rain, and snowstorms. But once the trees are logged off, many of these animals would be faced with the ultimatum: "Move elsewhere or die!" After all, how much food would a deer find on a bare patch of ground?

Chapter 4

Can Our Sick Earth Get Well?

Can our sick planet Earth continue to support the standard of living that America, Canada, and the other more developed countries (MDCs) enjoy, by the year 2000? What about the year 2050, when many of you readers probably will still be living? This important question is almost impossible to answer. That's because there are so many different factors involved. Among them are changing patterns of population, pollution, resource use, social attitudes, industrial production, international politics, and war and peace.

According to some pessimists, maintaining our present quality of life will be much more difficult than it was to develop the nuclear bomb or put a man on the moon. Several years ago, scientists at the Massachusetts Institute of Technology (MIT) tried to figure out what life would be like by the year 2050 if humans do not "nurse" the Earth's environment back to health. Their prediction? Shortly after 2050, well within your lifetime, hundreds of millions of people would starve to death because of a sharp decrease in food production. Even worse, they estimated that humanity would end by 2100. Why? Because the Earth's stock of resources would either have been destroyed by pollution or completely used up.

Many people criticize these pessimistic predictions. They are much more optimistic. They claim that new advances in technology will end all our population-pollution-resource problems. They believe that if enough energy is available, almost any environmental problem can be solved. Pollution would be controlled. Enough food could be produced to fill every human stomach. Even more, no one person on Earth would lack clothing and shelter. These optimists suggest that unlimited supplies of energy could be derived from nuclear power plants.

They have dreamed up many ways to increase the world's food supplies. These methods range from desert irrigation to fish farming, from draining swamps to breeding miracle wheat and giant corn. The optimists also claim that we can produce oil from worn out tires, get methane fuel from cow manure, and make building blocks from coal ash and broken glass.

Perhaps neither the pessimists or the optimists are correct. Perhaps the correct view concerning the future of humans on the planet Earth is that of the moderates—somewhere in between. The moderates are very concerned with our population-pollution-resource problems. But unlike the pessimists, they feel there is enough time to solve them. The moderates brand our society and those of the other MDCs (Canada, Japan, Germany, England, France, etc.) as *spendthrift societies.* After all, we are spending the Earth's resources and causing a very sick environment.

The moderates warn that we must change to a *sustainable* society that will conserve its resources. This society must use its resources on a sustainable, long-term basis. This means that, eventually, the MDCs will be forced to live much more simply. The emphasis on material wealth must end.

Our focus must shift from material goods to moral, intellectual and spiritual values. Such a simpler lifestyle would be much easier on our natural environment. It would even result in a richer, fuller, happier life than we have now. The simple life would make possible a huge redistribution of the world's resources so that the poor nations get their fair share.

Humanity's shift from a spendthrift to a sustainable society will be a difficult challenge. It will require highly coordinated efforts from people of many nations and from different walks of life, from grade schoolers to college professors.

What You Can Do
Encourage your parents to join one of the following organizations that are committed to certain aspects of a "steady-state" environment:

Center for Environmental Education, 624 Ninth Street North, Washington, D.C. 20001

Center for Planet Management, Box 541, Boulder, Colorado 80302

Citizens for a Better Environment, 33 East Congress, Suite 523, Chicago, Illinois 60605

Environmental Defense Fund, 444 Park Avenue South, New York, New York 10016

Friends of the Earth, 1045 Sansome Street, San Francisco, California 94111

Make your natural environment a part of you. Get interested in such activities as:

wild flowers and butterfly identification

bird watching

canoeing

wildlife photography

astronomy

Become politically involved. Do some "networking." Convince two friends, classmates or relatives to write letters to newspapers, city councils, state environmental agencies, state and federal legislators in which they express the need for our society to shift from a spendthrift to a steady-state condition. Have these people promise to get a commitment from two other persons. If this procedure of "doubling" is repeated only 28 times, every citizen in the United States will be aware of the importance of this crucial shift in the way we use our resources!

Glossary

Breeding potential—the ability of an organism to reproduce.

Carbon monoxide—a poisonous gas released when wood, coal, oil, gasoline, natural gas and other fuels are burned.

Cholera—a painful waterborne disease that causes cramps, vomiting, diarrhea and possibly death.

Dysentery—a waterborne disease that causes severe diarrhea.

Ecology—the study of the inter-relationships between organisms and their environment.

Emphysema—a condition in which the lungs lose their elasticity and have trouble exhaling carbon dioxide.

Environment—all the living and non-living surroundings of an organism.

Environmental science—the study of inter-relationships between organisms and their environment, with a major focus on humans.

Experiment—a step in the scientific method in which hypotheses are tested.

Exploitation—the overuse, misuse, waste and destruction of natural resources.

Extinction—the end of an organism's existence on Earth.

54

Fossil fuels—fuels like coal, oil and natural gas that were produced millions of year ago from dead plants and animals.

Hepatitis—a liver infection characterized by yellow skin, high fever and chocolate-colored urine.

Hypothesis—a step in the scientific method. A proposed explanation of something that is observed.

Landfill—a modern system of rubbish disposal in which the solid waste is covered with soil.

Market hunter—a hunter who kills large numbers of game for sale to the food industry.

Multiple use—the idea that a given resource, like a forest, may have uses, such as timber, erosion control, and habitats for wildlife.

Natural resources—any part of the world of nature that has value to humans.

Observation—the first step of the scientific method.

Pollution—the act of dirtying or degrading a natural resource so that it is less valuable to humans.

Preservation—an approach to resource management in which the original character of the resource is maintained.

Renewable resource—a resource such as soil, water, air, forests, fish, or wildlife, which can be renewed in a somewhat short time.

Science—knowledge based on observations and tested truths.

Sequoias—extremely tall evergreen trees that grow in California; some are more than 1,000 years old.

Solid waste—rubbish such as cans, bottles and tires.

Sulfur dioxide—a colorless gas released when sulfur containing fuels like coal, oil and natural gas are burned.

Projects

The Scientific Method

The Observation
You have casually seen sparrows around your home or feeding in your schoolyard. You noticed that they seemed to eat some kinds of foods while ignoring others.

The Hypothesis
Sparrows are selective about what they eat.

The Experiment
Select two identical cardboard boxtops that are about one foot square and are very shallow. Place them in the ground about five feet apart and close enough to your home so that you can see them from the windows. Scatter one cup of oatmeal in one tray and one cup of crushed popcorn in the other. In one hour, watch the food trays continuously for 30 minutes. Then record the following information:

The maximum number of birds seen on a given food tray at one time;

The total number of minutes a bird or birds were seen feeding at a given tray;

The total number of switches from one food tray to the other.

Conclusion
Based on the recorded data, conclude whether sparrows prefer oatmeal or popcorn. Hand in all your data and conclusions to your teacher.

Population Growth

Consult your county courthouse or reference librarian in your public library to find out the population of your town in 1940 and in 1990. Assume that this rate of increase continues until 2050, well within your lifetime. What will your town's population be in 2050?

Repeat this procedure for your country, and predict the population by 2050. Can you think of any serious environmental problems that might result from such population growth? With the aid of Target Earth™ Earthmobile books and additional material in your school or public libraries, find out some basic ways by which this population build-up can be brought under control.

Sample calculation
Your town's population in 1940 = 1,000.
Your town's population in 1990 = 2,000.
This is a 100% increase in 50 years, or a 2% increase per year.
A 2% increase = 40 people.
The population increase by 2050 will be 40 x 60 = 2,400.
2,000 + 2,400 = 4,400.
In the rare event that you town's population has decreased, use the same calculations but with negative percentages and rates.

Solid Waste

1) Collect the solid waste items (other than garbage) that your family accumulates over a one-week period.

2) Weigh the waste and record it.

3) How many newspaper pages, paper bags, plastic bags, and tin cans were in this waste?

4) How did your family dispose of this waste? Was it burned? Dumped? Recycled? Describe any other disposal methods.

5) Bring your information to class.

6) Using information from the other class members, figure out the total number of newspaper pages, paper bags, plastic bags, plastic bottles, glass bottles, aluminum cans and tin cans in the waste produced in one week by your classmates' families. What is the total weight of the trash? How many of these items would your classmates' families produce in one year? How much would one year's trash weigh?

Sediment Pollution

1) Select two identical small aquariums. Place fine gravel on the bottom. Supply with water and aerate.

2) Stock each aquarium with four small goldfish, four Elodea plants and four snails. (These are available at pet stores.)

3) On Day 1, empty one cup of clear water in aquarium A; empty one cup of very muddy water in aquarium B. How do the fish react in each aquarium?

4) On Day 2, record the following data for both aquariums:

__apparent vitality of the fish, snails and Elodea
__number of gill movements of the fish per minute
__swimming movements of the fish (vigorous, sluggish, non-
    existent)
__color of the Elodea
__number of oxygen bubbles on the Elodea

After recording your data, repeat the procedure of Day 1 as described in 3.

5) Continue this procedure for four consecutive days.

6) On the morning of Day 6, make your final set of observations as shown in 4.

7) Based on your observations, what are your conclusions about the effect of the sediment pollution on your goldfish, snails and Elodea? Many fish species spawn in weedbeds near the shore. How would sediment pollution affect their breeding success?

Pollution from Motor Vehicles

Check the odometer(s) of your parents' car(s). How many miles (km) has it (have they) been driven? How old is (are) the car(s)? Figure out the average number of miles (km) driven per year. Consult your state motor vehicle department to find out how many car licenses were issued for the past year for your town. Assume these cars averaged the same number of miles (km) as your parents' car(s).

Assume that all cars got 25 miles (10.627476 km) to the gallon (liter). How many gallons (liters) of gasoline were consumed by the cars in your town last year? Find out from the public library, or your local environmental protection agency, the kinds of pollutants and the total weight of each pollutant discharged from a car when it burns one gallon (liter) of unleaded gasoline.

Having an estimate of the total number of gallons (liters) of gasoline consumed by cars in your town last year, figure out the total tonnage (metric tonnage) of each type of pollutant released into the atmosphere of your town.

Sample Calculation

Assume the average number of miles (km) driven per car was 10,000 (16,090 km). Assume the total number of licenses issued last year was 250. The total number of miles (km) driven by cars in your town was:

> 10,000 miles (16,090 km) x 250 = 2,500,000 total miles (4,022,500 km) driven.

The total number of gallons (liters) of gas consumed was:

> 2,500,000 miles ÷ 25 miles per gallon = 100,000 gallons.
> (4,022,500 km ÷ 10.627476 km per liter = 378,500 liters.)

Suppose that when each gallon (liter) of gas is burned, the following weights of pollutants are released into the air:

- .5 oz. (14 grams) of sulfur dioxide (SO_2)   •(3.698811 grams per liter)
- 1.0 oz. (28 grams) of carbon monoxide (CO)   •(7.3976221 grams per liter)
- 3.0 oz. (84 grams) of carbon dioxide (CO_2)   •(22.192866 grams per liter)

Recall that:

- 16 oz. = 1 lb.   •(1,000 grams = 1 kg)
- 2,000 lbs. = 1 ton   •(1,000 kg = 1 metric ton)

The tonnage (metric tonnage) of each pollutant released into your town's air last year was:

sulfur dioxide
• .5 oz. in each gallon x 100,000 gallons of gasoline burned = 50,000 oz. of sulfur dioxide. 50,000 oz. ÷ 16 oz. = 3,125 lbs. ÷ 2,000 lbs. = 1.56 tons of sulfur dioxide in the air.

• (3.698811 grams in each liter x 378,500 liters of gasoline burned = 1,400,000 grams of sulfur dioxide. 1,400,000 grams ÷ 1,000 grams = 1,400 kilograms ÷ 1,000 kg = 1.4 metric tons of sulfur dioxide in the air.)

carbon monoxide
• 1 oz. in each gallon x 100,000 gallons of gasoline burned = 100,000 oz. of carbon monoxide. 100,000 oz. ÷ 16 oz. = 3.1 tons of sulfur dioxide in the air.

• (7.3976221 grams in each liter x 378,500 liters of gasoline burned = 2,800,000 grams of carbon monoxide. 2,800,000 grams ÷ 1,000 grams = 2,800 kilograms ÷ 1,000 kg = 2.8 metric tons of carbon monoxide in the air.)

carbon dioxide
• 3 oz. in each gallon x 100,000 gallons of gasoline burned = 300,000 oz. of carbon dioxide. 300,000 oz ÷ 16 oz. = 18,750 lbs ÷ 2,000 lbs. = 9.4 tons of carbon dioxide in the air.

• (22.192866 grams in each liter x 378,500 liters of gasoline burned = 8,400,000 grams of sulfur dioxide. 8,400,000 grams ÷ 1,000 grams = 8,400 kilograms ÷1,000 kg = 8.4 metric tons or carbon dioxide in the air.)

Endangered Species

Find out from your state conservation department office, or your local Sierra Club or Audubon Society, what species of animals are endangered near your city or town. With information from these and other sources (such as the public library), find out what caused the population decline of one of these species. Could the decline have been prevented? Describe the typical breeding sites for this species. What is their major type of food? Will these endangered species have the same fate as the passenger pigeon? Why or why not? Obtain khodochrome slides of several endangered animal species in your area. You can also use a video cassette from the public library, the state conservation department or your local Sierra Club or Audubon Society. With the aid of this material, present a brief presentation to the class on this subject.

Connect With Groups

The following agencies will be happy to send you free information on environmental problems and methods for their control:

- Council on Environmental Quality, 722 Jackson Place NW, Washington, DC 20006, (202) 395-5700.
- Agriculture Stabilization and Conservation Service, Washington, DC 20013.
- U.S. Forest Service, P.O. Box 2417, Washington, DC 20013, (202) 447-3957.
- National Marine Fisheries Service, U.S. Department of Commerce, NOAA, Washington, DC 20235.
- National Oceanic and Atmospheric Administration, Rockville, MD 20852, (301) 443-8910.
- Army Corps of Engineers, Office of the Chief of Engineers, Forrestal Building, Washington, DC 20314.
- Federal Energy Regulatory Commission, 825 N. Capitol St. NE, Washington, DC 20426.
- Food and Drug Administration, 5600 Fishers Lane, Rockville, MD 20857, (301) 443-1544.
- Bureau of Land Management, Washington, DC 20240, (202) 343 plus extension; information Ext. 1100.
- Bureau of Mines, Washington, DC 20241, (202) 634-1004.
- Bureau of Reclamation, Washington, DC 20240, (202) 343-4662.
- Geological Survey, National Center, Reston, VA 22092, (703) 860-7000.
- Office of Surface Mining, U.S. Department of the Interior, 1951 Constitution Avenue NW, Washington, DC 20240.
- Office of Water Research and Technology, Washington, DC 20240, (202) 343-4608.
- U.S. Fish and Wildlife Service, Washington, DC 20240.
- Urban Mass Transportation Administration, 400 Seventh Street SW, Washington, DC 20590, (202) 426-4043.
- Endangered Species Scientific Authority, 18th and C Streets NW, Washington, DC 20240, (202) 653-5948.
- Environmental Protection Agency, 401 M Street SW, Washington, DC 20460, (202) 382-3568.

Index

TARGET EARTH COMMITMENT

At Target, we're committed to the environment. We show this commitment not only through our own internal efforts but also through the programs we sponsor in the communities where we do business.

Our commitment to children and the environment began when we became the Founding International Sponsor for Kids for Saving Earth, a non-profit environmental organization for kids. We helped launch the program in 1989 and supported its growth to three-quarters of a million club members in just three years.

Our commitment to children's environmental education led to the development of an environmental curriculum called Target Earth, aimed at getting kids involved in their education and in their world.

In addition, we worked with Abdo & Daughters Publishing to develop the Target Earth Earthmobile, an environmental science library on wheels that can be used in libraries, or rolled from classroom to classroom.

Target believes that the children are our future and the future of our planet. Through education, they will save the world!

TARGET®

Minneapolis-based Target Stores is an upscale discount department store chain of 517 stores in 33 states coast-to-coast, and is the largest division of Dayton Hudson Corporation, one of the nation's leading retailers.